PRESENTED TO

HEAVEN
IS SO
REAL!
DEVOTIONAL

HEAVEN
IS SO
REAL!
DEVOTIONAL

Choo Thomas

Charisma
HOUSE
A STRANG COMPANY

Most STRANG COMMUNICATIONS/CHARISMA HOUSE/SILOAM/
FRONTLINE/REALMS products are available at special quantity dis-
counts for bulk purchase for sales promotions, premiums, fund-raising,
and educational needs. For details, write Strang Communications/
Charisma House/Siloam/FrontLine/Realms, 600 Rinehart Road,
Lake Mary, Florida 32746, or telephone (407) 333-0600.

HEAVEN IS SO REAL! DEVOTIONAL by Choo Thomas
Published by Charisma House
A Strang Company
600 Rinehart Road
Lake Mary, Florida 32746
www.charismahouse.com

Unless otherwise noted, all Scripture quotations are from New King
James Version of the Bible. Copyright © 1979, 1980, 1982 by Thomas
Nelson, Inc., publishers. Used by permission.

Interior design by Terry Clifton

Library of Congress Cataloging-in-Publication Data
Thomas, Choo.
  Heaven is so real devotional / Choo Thomas. -- 1st ed.
    p. cm.
  ISBN 1-59979-017-3 (casebound)
  1. Heaven--Christianity--Meditations. 2. Meditations. I. Title.
  BT846.3.T46 2006
  242--dc22

                    2006019013
            ISBN-13: 978-1-59979-017-6
                    First Edition
            06 07 08 09 10 — 987654321
        Printed in the United States of America

CONTENTS

PART III: ANOINTED FOR MINISTRY

INTRODUCTION

When I received the prophetic utterance from Pastor Larry Randolph in 1995 that God would speak to me through dreams and visions, my heart soared, but my mind tried to find its way into the old channel of questioning because I felt so unworthy to receive such a wonderful personal message and calling. *How can God use me?* I thought. *I am a Korean American, and my use of the English language is not as proficient as it should be. Why would God pick me to be His friend? Why me?*

Then I remembered the words of one of my favorite verses: "Trust in the LORD with all your heart, and lean not on your own understanding; in all your ways acknowledge Him, and He shall direct your paths" (Prov. 3:5–6). Little did I realize where those paths would lead me, but I was firm in my resolve to trust the Lord without leaning on my own understanding. After all, isn't this the essence of the spiritual life? We're spiritual beings on a human journey.

This book will mean nowhere near as much to you as I believe it could if you haven't first read *Heaven Is So Real!*, the work on which this one is based. In that book I struggled to put down everything I had seen, heard, and felt in the presence of my beloved Savior, Jesus Christ of Nazareth. He literally took me to heaven with Him on numerous occasions over the course of several months to share with me things that He clearly wanted me to pass on to others.

These encounters were not imaginary, they were not illusions, and most of all, they were not encounters that I initiated on my own or even wished for—at least in the beginning. Let me repeat a small portion of my preface to *Heaven Is So Real!* to show you what I mean:

In this book I will be sharing with you the experiences I have had in heaven with Jesus. From the outset, I want you to understand the circumstances surrounding each of these visits to heaven.

A passage from the first letter by the apostle Paul to the Christians in ancient Corinth will help make this clear. It says:

> Behold, I tell you a mystery: We shall not all sleep, but we shall all be changed—in a moment, in the twinkling of an eye, at the last trumpet. For the trumpet will sound, and the dead will be raised incorruptible, and we shall be changed. For this corruptible must put on incorruption, and this mortal must put on immortality. So when this corruptible has put on incorruption, and this mortal has put on immortality…then shall be brought to pass the saying that is written: "Death is swallowed up in victory."
> —1 Corinthians 15:51–54

This periscope of Scripture refers to the End Times, when those who know the Lord will go to be with Him forever. When this happens, we will have to exchange our mortal bodies for incorruptible, heavenly bodies.

Every time I have gone to heaven with Jesus this exchange actually has occurred. God would give me a new body—a body in which I looked remarkably like I did when I was a teenager. Each time the transformation would take place at a beach on earth, and then He escorted me to heaven. Other times I would be clothed in my incorruptible body in my bedroom at home.

People often ask me, "Were your experiences in heaven like visions or dreams, or did you actually go there?" My only response to these questions is that I know I've seen heaven, and I know that *heaven is so real*. Whether we place my experiences in the category of supernatural dreams, visions, or actual experiences, I will leave to the theologians. All I can say is that they were very real to me.

It never ceases to amaze me that the Lord has called me to write down my experiences with Him and take His message to everyone. As I said earlier, I am a Korean American whose use of the English language is somewhat limited. Nonetheless, the Lord chose me to do His work. He told me to tell everything I experienced and heard, and that was the purpose of writing the book.

The idea for this devotional book arose from numerous requests, from readers all over the world, for something beyond the first book that would help them "stay connected" to the experiences they shared with me while reading *Heaven Is So Real!* They did not want that sharing to end, and quite frankly, neither did I. God always has more for us than we can glean from a first encounter, a first reading, and even a firsthand experience with anything He puts in front of us.

I believe that's why my original conviction, that God had charged me to tell others about my own experiences with Him, has been repeatedly verified—and strengthened—by the reactions of so many readers. One of my major concerns when I first began to write *Heaven Is So Real!* was to keep myself firmly anchored in the center of God's will, consistently responding to *His leading only*, so that everything I wrote would reflect His desires, His will, and His directions rather than my own. I was the conduit, He was the Source, and that's the way it must always be.

Given all that, the present devotional book, based on the original text of *Heaven Is So Real!*, was both the logical and the spiritual successor of that first book. So, let me give you two or three additional insights into how the structure of that book corresponds and reinforces the structure of this book.

Then let me conclude by offering a few suggestions on how you might use this book in your own devotional life.

Reading Through the Devotional

Initially, the purpose of this devotional was to provide a series of links back to the original book that would help you, the reader, focus your own daily meditations and prayers on the specific concepts and concerns that we all shared while writing and reading *Heaven Is So Real!* Thus, nothing we have included in this book was or is "written in stone" in the sense that we thought it might be timeless or especially worthy because of its own merit. But the animating spirit behind *Heaven Is So Real! was* and *is* the Holy Spirit, and that made every other consideration fall into second place.

As I have said so many times already, I was not responsible for originating many of those thoughts, and I was not responsible for gaining by myself the opportunities to observe some of the things of God—especially of heaven!—that were put in front of me. That, of course, is truly the only basis on which I can recommend them to you.

As you may remember, the first book was organized into three separate sections, as follows:

> Part One: Visitations and Visions
> Part Two: Preparation and Anointing
> Part Three: Three Years of Ministry Training

This book is also organized into three separate sections, with slightly different titles. These current sections correspond somewhat to the original ones, but not precisely.

The reason is quite simple. The entries for this book focus more on the first section than sections two and three, because the first section concentrated more on the background for all that followed. It focused more on my own learning experiences. Thus it dealt with many of the lessons I had to learn in the beginning, and I had many such lessons to embrace—as do many other people as well.

To put that another way, I believe that what I needed to learn will probably resonate quite powerfully with many of you, my readers, because I think many of us fervently desire daily, intimate contact with God—a true, interactive relationship. Yet we always have so much more to learn about how to have a relationship with Him.

One of the features you will find at the end of each section is pages to record your own encounters with the Lord. After I experienced the marvelous encounters with Him, I would usually lie in bed and reflect on the wonderful experiences I just saw and lived. Then I would write those experiences in my journal. You will find journal pages at the end of each section so that you too can record your experiences with our Lord's presence.

As You Begin Your Own Spiritual Journey

In closing, I ask only that you receive the contents of this devotional in the same way it was written—with total openness to the Lord and His will. As you read each entry, some basic principles will surely apply.

1. I would encourage you to set aside a daily time for your own personal devotions—your own private time with God. I'm sure you're already doing it, but just in case, hear the suggestion again.

2. Use this book as an "extra" or a "helper" text only. The Bible itself is the only indispensable book,

and it must not be pushed aside by any other book no matter how "relevant" or "useful" another one might seem. Evaluate my experiences in the light of God's Word.

3. I would always encourage you to remember that anything from someone such as me, human as I am, can never be perfect. It can never replace your own experience with God; it can never serve as a guidebook more fitting for your life; it can never substitute for what you can gain by focusing, praying, and reading directly "on," "to," and "of" Him alone.

He alone is our Savior, our Guide, and our King. How thankful I am that I have been privileged to have this foretaste of glory so I can share it with you. God wants me to let you know that He already has prepared a place for you in heaven if you only will believe in His Son and receive Him as your personal Lord and Savior.

My prayer for you is that you will catch more than a glimpse of heaven as you read and that you will be changed—as I was—and experience the security of knowing Jesus has already prepared a place for you and your loved ones. Yes, *heaven is so real!*

—Choo Thomas
Tacoma, Washington

Part One

VISIONS AND VISITATIONS

THE WEIGHT...OF THE WAIT

Wait on the LORD; be of good courage, and He shall strengthen your heart; wait, I say, on the LORD!

—PSALM 27:14

Heavenly Father, may all my moments of waiting move me to moments of service in Your glorious name . . .

The presence of the Lord was so real I felt like I could have reached out and held His hand. I was feeling a spiritual reality, but it far exceeded anything I had ever experienced in the natural realm.

There was an expectancy in my heart. Somehow I realized that all I needed to do was to continue waiting in the presence of the Lord, and He would speak to me and show me wonderful things.

Waiting—one of the hardest things in the world to do, and yet the key to so much empowerment in the spiritual realm. The Lord wants us to wait in His presence, because this is how we develop the patience we need to grow and to serve.

TO REACH THE BEGINNING, WE FEAR

"Do you not fear Me?" says the LORD. "Will you not tremble at My presence?"

—JEREMIAH 5:22

❧

Sometimes the anointing of God was so heavy on me that I felt as if I would faint. At other times it would leave me feeling dizzy and weak. Often I would lay in bed completely immobilized by the overpowering presence of God.

Strangely, I didn't find any of this the least bit unusual. The Bible is replete with examples of people quaking and shaking in the presence of the Lord. Sometimes this manifestation is accompanied by fear, but most of the time it is preparatory.

God is about to do a great work through a yielded vessel.

Dear Lord, I pray that my fear of You might be the awe that leads to knowledge and understanding, but even more to the application of Your wisdom as I follow in Your footsteps . . .

Dearest Jesus,
might all that
comes from my
heart be focused
on You, and
all that comes
from my efforts
in Your behalf
be in service
to the unique
purpose You
have established
for my life . . .

THE GREATEST CHOICE OF ALL

You did not choose Me, but I chose you and appointed you that you should go and bear fruit, and that your fruit should remain, that whatever you ask the Father in My name He may give you.

—JOHN 15:16

God had chosen me for a specific work. It was too wonderful to imagine, and yet it was exciting beyond words.

The Lord had chosen me to go and bear lasting fruit. This is what I wanted than anything in the world. His Word, His presence, His anointing confirmed His calling in my life. I committed my heart to obeying the Lord from that moment on, no matter what the consequences.